D0561405

To _____

From _____

Never Let It End

POEMS OF A LIFELONG LOVE

RUTH BELL GRAHAM

Baker Books

A Division of Baker Book House Co
Grand Rapids, Michigan 49516

FOREWORD

*T*hese poems remind me of the time I visited and had a rare and precious opportunity to see a couple who have loved and lost, triumphed and failed—all of those things, together, in one flesh.

One of the things I saw in that brief interlude with them is that they both had tremendous wills. They are both strong. Can you imagine Dr. Billy Graham being married to a weak woman? I cannot. It would have taken the forces of heaven itself to have the patience to raise all of those extraordinary children, largely in Billy's absence, and to run that place single-handed.

I saw them tease each other and I saw how merciless both he and she could be, and how they loved it. I saw how they held hands, how they looked fondly at one another, how they laughed.

She talked about their walks. I could see them walking down that long, winding, wonderful mountain trail together, holding hands. He has the most gorgeous hands—long tapered fingers—the hands of a great pianist holding her tiny, hummingbird hands.

I just thought they were the cutest, sexiest couple I had ever seen.

JAN KARON

PREFACE

I read my old premarriage poems, among the later ones included in this volume, with a bit of amusement. I wrote them so earnestly—meaning every word—and lived to find them really unfair.

Pity the married couple who expect too much from one another.

It is a foolish woman who expects her husband to be to her that which only Jesus Christ Himself can be: always ready to forgive, totally understanding, unendingly patient, invariably tender and loving, unfailing in every area, anticipating every need, and making more than adequate provision. Such expectations put a man under an impossible strain. The same goes for the man who expects too much from his wife.

RUTH GRAHAM

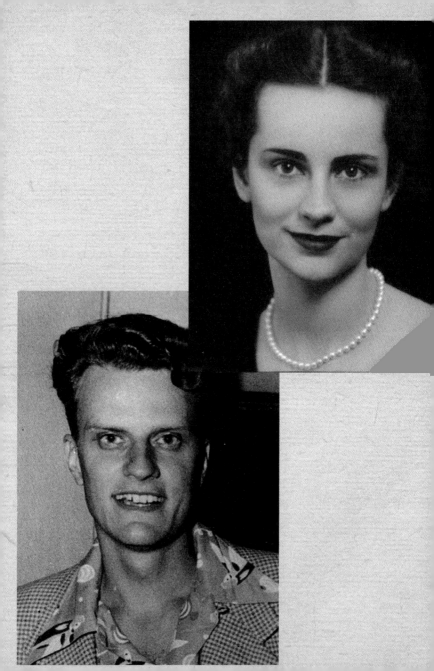

From the time I was a very small girl, I knew that my mother and daddy loved each other. It was obvious.

GIGI GRAHAM TCHIVIDJIAN

Dear God, I prayed, all unafraid
(as we're inclined to do),
I do not need a handsome man
but let him be like You;
I do not need one big and strong
nor yet so very tall,
nor need he be some genius,
or wealthy, Lord, at all;
but let his head be high, dear God,
and let his eye be clear,
his shoulders straight, whate'er his state,
whate'er his earthly sphere;
and let his face have character,
a ruggedness of soul,
and let his whole life show, dear God,
a singleness of goal;
then when he comes
(as he will come)
with quiet eyes aglow,
I'll understand that he's the man
I prayed for long ago.

———✻———

Your eyes
look down at me
so thoughtfully . . .
What do they see?
The plainness of me—
plainly built,
not small,
nor calmly poised,
nor quaint,
and, worst of all,
a nose upturned
and hands
that I have known
for years to be
too long,
too overgrown;

plain hazel eyes,
a face too pale,
not fair,
a mouth too large
and ordinary hair?
And all of me
tucked in
this homemade dress;
oh, if you look at me
so thoughtfully,
will you love me
the less?

I looked into your face and knew
   that you were true;
those clear, deep eyes awoke in me
   a trust in you.

I'd dreamt of shoulders broad and straight,
   one built to lead;
I met you once and knew that you
   were all I need.

You did not have to say a word
   to make me feel
that will, completely in control,
   was made of steel.

I'd dreamt of dashing love and bold,
    life wild with zest;
but when with you my heart was stilled
    to perfect rest.

And how? I could not understand,
    it seemed so odd:
till on my heart it quietly dawned
    —love is of God!

Each time Daddy entered the room, Mother's eyes lit up and I knew that she felt her heart "rise within her." He was quick to hold her close, grasp her hand or give her a tender kiss. It was clear to all that they adored one another and were in love.

GIGI GRAHAM TCHIVIDJIAN

———❦———

You held my hand
and I,
feeling a strange,
sweet thrill,
gave to my heart
a sharp rebuke,
and told it
to be still.

You held me close
and I
gasped, "Oh, no!"
until
I felt my heart within me rise
and tell me
to be still.

Years before, Mother had prayed that God would let her be all that Daddy ever dreamed of, that He would "make her strong, a help to him" and that she would be "worthy to be his wife."

GIGI GRAHAM TCHIVIDJIAN

Train our love
that it may grow
slowly . . . deeply . . . steadily;
till our hearts will overflow
unrestrained and readily.

Discipline it, too,
dear God;
strength of steel
throughout the whole.
Teach us patience,
thoughtfulness,
tenderness, and
self-control.

Deepen it
throughout the years,
age and mellow it
until, time that finds us
old without,
within,
will find us
lovers still.

Dear one,
I was cross last night
and you had worked
so hard all day.
Quietly you said, "Good night,"
closed the door,
and went away.

Nights can be
so very long
when hearts are far
that should be near;
I cannot wait
for day to come
and hear you say
"Good morning,
Dear."

———❧———

God, make me worthy to be his wife:
as cliffs are made, so make me strong,
a help for him when things go wrong.
Clear as the dew, Lord, make my mind,
clear as the dew, and just as kind;
and let me be refreshing too,
—and quiet to remind you
with him to laugh in face of tears,
in face of worries and of fears;
brave to be and do and bear,
quick to yield and glad to share.
Let him know through coming days
my love is warm for him always.
His head's held high as he faces life;
God, make me worthy to be his wife.

—⚘—

God,
let me be all he ever dreamed
of loveliness and laughter.
Veil his eyes a bit
because
there are so many little flaws;
somehow, God,
please let him see
only the bride I long to be,
remembering ever after—
I was all he ever dreamed
of loveliness and laughter.

Mother and Daddy come from quite different backgrounds. Daddy was raised on a North Carolina dairy farm and Mother thousands of miles away in China. They have very different personalities, strengths, ideas, and ways of doing things. But, Mother is fond of saying, "if two people agree on everything, one of them is unnecessary."

GIGI GRAHAM TCHIVIDJIAN

"With this ring . . ."
your strong, familiar voice
fell like a benediction
on my heart, that dusk;
tall candles flickered gently,
our age-old vows were said,
and I could hear
someone begin to sing
an old, old song,
timeworn and lovely,
timeworn and dear.
And in that dusk
were old, old friends—
and you,
an old friend, too,
(and dearer than them all).

Only my ring seemed new—
its plain gold surface
warm and bright
and strange to me
that candlelight . . .
unworn—unmarred
Could it be that wedding rings
like other things,
are lovelier when scarred?

Dear Lord,
we've built this little house
with sloping eaves, and windows wide,
gray stone walls, and rustic doors,
and paneled all inside.

We've prayed
and planned and built this house.
And here we pause, for You alone
can by Your presence hallow it
and make this house a home.

Ours is a little home
newly begun.
So, we would ask of Thee,
Lord, let it always be
chock-full of fun.

Homes, even newest ones,
often are full of
things unexpected, gray;
so let it be always
bursting with love.

This, and above it all,
one special plea:
'mid outward storms, still it
and storm or calm, fill it,
Lord, full of Thee.

It was so very good of God
to let my dreams come true,
to note a young girl's cherished hopes,
then lead her right to you;
so good of Him to take such care
in little, detailed parts
(He knows how much details mean
to young and wishful hearts);
so good of Him to let you be
tall and slender, too,
with waving hair more blond than brown
and eyes of steel blue.

Daddy was gone much of the time and Mother missed him terribly although she never complained. There were times when it was so difficult to be separated that she slept with one of his jackets.

GIGI GRAHAM TCHIVIDJIAN

Leave a little light on
somewhere, in some room,
dark, rainy days;
where, in the deepening gloom,
I, damped and grayed
by weather, might
in some unexpected place
glimpse warmth and cheer.
Those who feel that light
is utilitarian only,
have never known
the desolation dusk can bring,
to being lonely.

I need Your help
in the evening
more, I think,
than at dawn.
For tiredness comes
with twilight,
and my resolves are gone.
I'm thinking of rest
not service,
of valleys
instead of steeps,
and my dreams are not
of conquest
but the blissful oblivion
of sleep.

When the day approached that
Daddy was due back home,
Mother would visibly brighten
and with excitement begin
to prepare herself and the house
for his homecoming assuring
him that "her love was warm
for him always."

GIGI GRAHAM TCHIVIDJIAN

Never let it end, God,
never—please—
all this growing loveliness,
all of these
brief moments of
fresh pleasure—
never let it end.
Let us always
be a little breathless
at love's beauty;
never let us
pause to reason
from a sense of duty;

never let us
stop to measure
just how much to give;
never let us
stoop to weigh love;
let us live—
and live!
Please, God,
let our hearts kneel always,
Love their only master,
knowing the warm impulsiveness
of shattered alabaster:
I know You can see things
the way a new bride sees,
so
never let it end, God,
never—please.

When Daddy had to leave again, Mother (a true example of "love without clinging") would summon the grace of an uncommon strength, and with tears in her eyes, kiss him good-bye. We all stood outside and waved as Daddy's car made its way down the long driveway. When it rounded the last curve, Mother, sensing our sadness, would push her own feelings and emotions aside to take our minds off Daddy's departure. "Well," she would say, "let's clean the attic" or "let's go to the pound for a new dog or kitten."

As I grew older I realized that my parents' love for one another was deeper than just the look in their eyes each time one of them came into the room. Their love was based on more than their physical and emotional attraction. It was based on solid, uncompromising commitment—first to Jesus Christ, second to the institution of marriage (Mother has teasingly said, "Divorce never, murder maybe"), and then commitment to each other.

GIGI GRAHAM TCHIVIDJIAN

When
in the morning
I make our bed,
pulling his sheets
and covers tight,
I know the tears
I shouldn't shed
will fall unbidden
as the rain;
and I would kneel,
praying again
words I mean
but cannot feel.

"Lord,
not my will
but Thine
be done."
The doubts dissolving
one by one . . .
For I will realize as I pray,
that's why it happened
. . . and this way.

Sometimes, unobserved by us, there were disagreements. Afterward, Mother would share with her pen, "nights can be so very long when hearts are far that should be near." However, Mother and Daddy have allowed their differences to strengthen their relationship.

Gigi Graham Tchividjian

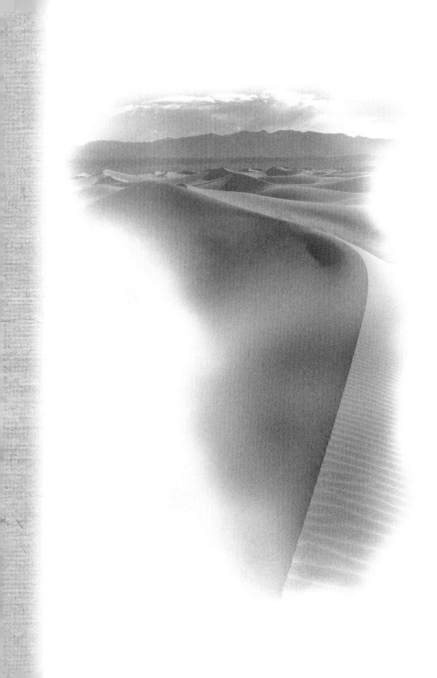

———※———

Why
argue
and fight,
and worry
how the world ends?
Pray for the best,
prepare for the worst,
and take whatever God sends.

The little things that bug me,
resentments deep within;
the things I ought to do, undone,
the irritations one by one
till nerves stretch screaming-thin
and bare for all the world to see—
which needs His touch to make it whole
the most, my body or my soul?

I pray—nothing comes out right,
my thoughts go flying everywhere;
my attitudes are all confused,
I hate myself—I am not used
to hands all clenched, not clasped, in prayer,
and heart too leaden to take flight;
which, oh, which needs to be whole
the most, my body or my soul?

I cannot read, I cannot pray.
I cannot even think.
Where to from here? And how get there
with only darkness everywhere?
I ought to rise and sink . . .
and feel His arms, and hear Him say,
"I love you." It was all my soul
or body needed to be whole.

You look at me
and see
my flaws;
I look at you
and see flaws, too.
Those who love,
know love
deserves
a second glance;
each failure serves
another chance.
Love looks to see,
beyond the scars
and flaws,
the cause;
and scars become
an honorable badge
of battles fought
and won—
(or lost) but fought!

The product,
not the cost,
is what love sought.

***

God help us see
beyond the now
to the before,
and note with tenderness
what lies between
—and love the more!

They not only share a deep love for one another, but a mutual respect. In the early years, Daddy made decisions without consulting Mother and then expected her to follow. With a mischievous twinkle in her eyes, she said, "There comes a time to quit submitting and start outwitting." She has done her share of both. But, Mother and Daddy have given each other space in their marriage to pursue the gifts and callings from God.

GIGI GRAHAM TCHIVIDJIAN

—— ✿ ——

We live a time
secure;
beloved and loving,
sure
it cannot last
for long
then—
the good-byes come
again—again—
like a small death,
the closing of a door.

One learns to live
with pain.
One looks ahead,
not back—
never back,
only before.
And joy will come again—
warm and secure,
if only for the now,
laughing,
we endure.

———❦———

Love
without clinging;
cry
if you must—
but privately cry;
the heart will adjust
to the newness of loving
in practical ways:
cleaning
and cooking
and sorting out clothes,
all say, "I love you,"
when lovingly done.

So—
love
without clinging;
cry—
if you must—
but privately cry;
the heart will adjust
to the length of his stride,
the song he is singing,
the trail he must ride,
the tensions that make him
the man that he is,
the world he must face,
the life that is his.

So
love
without clinging;
cry—
if you must—
but privately cry;
the heart will adjust
to being the heart,
not the forefront of life;
a part of himself,
not the object—
his wife.

So—
love!

———✶———

Never turn your back
on tears,
do not stem the flow;
put your arms about her
gently,
let her go.

Knowing why
is not important,
weeping
sometimes is.
Let her cry
—but kindly—
with a kiss.

A few years ago, a magazine dedicated an entire issue to the greatest love stories of recent years. Many celebrity marriages were featured, although most had crumbled already or the marriages ended in divorce. My parents were mentioned in a small insignificant corner. I couldn't help but think that of all the love stories featured, theirs was one that stood the test and survived —a real love story.

GIGI GRAHAM TCHIVIDJIAN

Now that I love you and see with eyes
by love enlightened and made wise,
I wonder how men look at you
who do not see you as I do?
They see (they must) the fire and steel,
the driving force I also feel.

But do they ever, ever see
that gentler side revealed to me?
That wealth of tenderness
man stores within his heart
from other men and guards,
and keeps and then outpours
when with the woman he adores?

Recently, Mother was in the hospital. Daddy, also frail and not well, came to visit. I stood back and observed these two very dear lovers as he entered the room. Her eyes once again lit up. As he made his way to her bedside, he tottered and almost lost his balance. Leaning over, he bent down and gently, tenderly kissed her. It was obvious that her desire and prayer as a young bride to "never let it end, God, never" had been answered.

GIGI GRAHAM TCHIVIDJIAN

When my Fall comes
I wonder
Will I feel
as I feel now?
glutted with happy memories,
content
to let them lie
like nuts
stored up against the coming cold?
Squirrels always gather
so I'm told
more than they will ever need;
and so have I.

Will the dry,
bitter smell of Fall,
the glory of the
dying leaves,
the last brave rose
against the wall,
fill me with quiet ecstasy
as they do now?

Will my thoughts turn
without regret,
to the warm comforts
Winter brings
of hearth fires,
books,
and inner things
and find them nicer yet?

The night Bill told me
he loved me,
what
did he discuss?
Us?
No.
   Emily!
   Beautiful.
   Sweet.
   Talented.
   Spiritual.
   (And second cousin to Herbert Hoover!)
I got madder,
(not sadder)
just madder and madder,
till blam!
with a slam
we rammed
into a truck
(what luck!).
(He was so busy looking
back he couldn't see where

he was going. There's a
moral here, but we won't
belabor it.)
Still,
there were no quarrels
thanks to Charles!

I met her
years later
and knew
I would
hate her:
I hoped,
without praying
(that goes
without saying),
but I hoped
(how I hoped!)
by now
she'd become
fat and dumb.

Well?
She was a doll!
What's more,
after all,
I liked her!
She'd earned all those laurels.
Still,
Thank you, Charles!

Thus
by the happy twists
of life
folks pair off
as man and wife,
and children come
to bless each home:

> Gigi
> Charles
> Anne
> Caroline
> Bunny

Joyce
Franklin
David
Ned

This is the moral
of my ode
(if this is an ode,
and if odes have morals):
Thank you, Charles!

My love has long been yours . . .
since on that day
when we first met—
I will never quite forget
how you just paused
and smiled a bit,
then calmly helped yourself to it.

With heartfelt emotion trying
to keep the tears from spilling
over I observed once again what
I had been privileged to observe
for more than half a century,
my parents lovers still.

GIGI GRAHAM TCHIVIDJIAN

A little more time,
Lord,
just a little more time.
There's so much to do,
so much undone.
If it's all right with You,
Lord,
please stop the sun.
There's forever before me
forever with You;
but a little more time
for the so much to do.

I met you years ago
when
of all the men
I knew,
you,
I hero-worshiped
then:
you are my husband now,
my husband!
and from my home
(your arms),
I turn to look
down the long trail of years
to where I met you first
and hero-worshiped,
and I would smile;
. . . I know you better now:
the faults,
the odd preferments,

the differences
that make you you.
That other me
—so young,
so far away—
saw you
and hero-worshiped
but never knew;
while I,
grown wiser
with the closeness of these years,
hero-worship, too!

And when I die
I hope my soul ascends
slowly, so that I
may watch the earth receding
out of sight,
its vastness growing smaller
as I rise,
savoring its recession
with delight.
Anticipating joy
is itself a joy.
And joy unspeakable
and full of glory
needs more
than "in the twinkling of an eye,"
more than "in a moment."

Lord, who am I to disagree?
It's only we
have much to leave behind;
so much . . . Before.
These moments
of transition
will, for me, be
time
to adore.

INDEX OF FIRST LINES

© 2001 by Ruth Bell Graham

Published by Baker Books
a division of Baker Book House Company
P.O. Box 6287, Grand Rapids, MI 49516–6287

Printed in the United States of America

Library of Congress Cataloging-in-Publication Data

Graham, Ruth Bell
   Never let it end: poems of a lifelong love
    ISBN: 0-8010-1207-4
     1. Marriage—Poetry. 2. Love poetry, American. 3. Christian poetry, American. I. Never Let It End: Poems of a Lifelong Love

PS3557.R222 N48 2001
811'.54—dc21   00-049794

For current information about all releases from Baker Book House, visit our web site:

              http://www.bakerbooks.com

Interior design by Brian Brunsting